PREDATORS

POLAR BEARS

BY MELISSA ROSS

WWW.APEXEDITIONS.COM

Copyright © 2024 by Apex Editions, Mendota Heights, MN 55120. All rights reserved. No part of this book may be reproduced or utilized in any form or by any means without written permission from the publisher.

Apex is distributed by North Star Editions:
sales@northstareditions.com | 888-417-0195

Produced for Apex by Red Line Editorial.

Photographs ©: Shutterstock Images, cover, 1, 4–5, 6, 8, 10–11, 12–13, 14–15, 16–17, 18, 19, 21, 22–23, 24–25, 26, 27, 29; iStockphoto, 7, 20

Library of Congress Control Number: 2023910145

ISBN
978-1-63738-774-0 (hardcover)
978-1-63738-817-4 (paperback)
978-1-63738-898-3 (ebook pdf)
978-1-63738-860-0 (hosted ebook)

Printed in the United States of America
Mankato, MN
012024

NOTE TO PARENTS AND EDUCATORS

Apex books are designed to build literacy skills in striving readers. Exciting, high-interest content attracts and holds readers' attention. The text is carefully leveled to allow students to achieve success quickly. Additional features, such as bolded glossary words for difficult terms, help build comprehension.

CHAPTER 1
SEA BEAR 4

CHAPTER 2
AN ICY HOME 10

CHAPTER 3
ARCTIC HUNTER 16

CHAPTER 4
LIFE CYCLE 22

COMPREHENSION QUESTIONS • 28
GLOSSARY • 30
TO LEARN MORE • 31
ABOUT THE AUTHOR • 31
INDEX • 32

CHAPTER 1

SEA BEAR

A polar bear lifts its head and sniffs. It smells a seal. The polar bear follows the scent to the edge of the ice.

A polar bear's large paws spread out its weight. It can walk on ice and snow without breaking through.

Polar bears eat several different kinds of seals.

The bear lies on a floating sheet of ice. It waits. Suddenly, the seal comes up for air. The polar bear's sharp claws grab the seal and pull it onto the ice.

FAST FACT

Polar bears can smell seals up to 20 miles (32 km) away.

Seals sometimes rest on the ice.

The polar bear bites into its **prey**. It eats the seal's skin and **blubber**. Then the polar bear takes a nap.

A POWERFUL BITE

A polar bear's mouth has 42 teeth. The front teeth have sharp points. They tear and grab prey. The teeth in the back chew and shred.

 Sometimes polar bears eat only part of their prey. They save the rest for later.

CHAPTER 2

AN ICY HOME

Polar bears are some of the largest land **carnivores** on Earth. They can grow up to 10 feet (3 m) tall.

Male polar bears can weigh more than 1,700 pounds (770 kg).

Polar bears live in the **Arctic**. Temperatures there are below freezing. In winter, polar bears live on large sheets of ice.

FAST FACT

Polar bears can hold their breath for more than a minute.

Polar bears are strong swimmers. They can swim for hours at a time.

A polar bear's fur helps it blend in with ice and snow.

Polar bears have a thick layer of blubber. This fat keeps them warm. Their fur helps, too. It has two layers. One layer traps heat. The other **repels** water.

SEE-THROUGH FUR

Polar bears have black skin. Scientists believe it helps soak up sunlight. The bears' fur is see-through. The hollow hairs reflect light. That makes polar bears look white.

CHAPTER 3

ARCTIC HUNTER

Polar bears are at the top of the Arctic **food chain**. They have no natural **predators**. Seals are their most common prey.

Polar bears can eat up to 150 pounds (68 kg) of food at once.

A polar bear might wait hours or days to catch a single seal.

When they are not sleeping, polar bears spend most of their time hunting. They can swim more than 60 miles (97 km) to find food.

BIG POLAR PAWS

Polar bear paws are the size of dinner plates. When a bear swims, its front paws work like paddles. The back paws help the bear steer.

Pads on a bear's paws help it balance on ice.

Polar bears usually eat meat. But sometimes they eat plant-like foods such as kelp.

Sometimes, polar bears can't catch enough seals. So, they eat other animals instead. They might eat animals such as reindeer, fish, or birds.

FAST FACT

Polar bears do not **hibernate** like some other bears. They hunt all year long.

Polar bears can jump between pieces of ice.

CHAPTER 4

LIFE CYCLE

Most polar bears live alone unless they are raising families. Bears find **mates** in the spring. Males follow the scents of females.

Polar bear mates usually stay together for about a week.

Female bears give birth eight months later. Each female usually has one to three cubs. At first, the cubs stay with the mother in a den.

MAMA BEAR

Polar bears dig dens in large piles of snow. A female enters her den in fall to give birth. She and the cubs stay inside until spring. She doesn't eat or drink that whole time.

When they are born, polar bear cubs weigh about 1 pound (0.5 kg). But they grow quickly.

Cubs drink their mother's milk for their first few months. After that, they can have solid food, too.

After three months, mothers start teaching the cubs to hunt. Cubs grow for two to three years. Then they are ready to live on their own.

FAST FACT Polar bears usually live 20 to 25 years in the wild.

Most polar bears begin having their own babies between ages 5 and 10.

COMPREHENSION QUESTIONS

Write your answers on a separate piece of paper.

1. Write a few sentences explaining how polar bears hunt seals.

2. Polar bears live in very cold temperatures. Would you like to live in the Arctic? Why or why not?

3. When do female polar bears leave their dens?
   - A. in spring
   - B. in fall
   - C. in winter

4. Why would it be useful for polar bears' skin to soak up sunlight?
   - A. It helps them get tanned.
   - B. It helps them stay warm.
   - C. It helps them stand out from the ice.

5. What does **dens** mean in this book?

*Polar bears dig **dens** in large piles of snow. A female enters her den in fall to give birth.*

    A. homes animals live in
    B. small holes in the ice
    C. places to store food

6. What does **hollow** mean in this book?

*The bears' fur is see-through. The **hollow** hairs reflect light. That makes polar bears look white.*

    A. black
    B. thick
    C. empty

Answer key on page 32.

GLOSSARY

Arctic
An area in the far northern part of the world that is very cold.

blubber
A thick layer of fat.

carnivores
Animals that eat meat.

food chain
A list showing which animals eat others in a habitat.

hibernate
To rest or sleep through the winter.

mates
Pairs of animals that come together to have babies.

predators
Animals that hunt and eat other animals.

prey
An animal that is hunted and eaten by another animal.

repels
Keeps something out or away.

BOOKS

Downs, Kieran. *Polar Bear vs. Walrus*. Minneapolis: Bellwether Media, 2022.

Easton, Marilyn. *Hot and Cold Animals: Sun Bear or Polar Bear*. New York: Scholastic, 2022.

Murray, Julie. *Polar Bears*. Minneapolis: Abdo Publishing, 2020.

ONLINE RESOURCES

Visit **www.apexeditions.com** to find links and resources related to this title.

ABOUT THE AUTHOR

Melissa Ross is the author of *Forensics for Kids* and other educational books for children. She is fascinated by the interesting animals we share our planet with, and she enjoys sharing the wonder of them with young readers.

INDEX

A
Arctic, 12, 16

B
blubber, 9, 15

C
cubs, 24, 26

D
dens, 24

F
fur, 15

H
hunting, 18, 21, 26

I
ice, 4, 6, 12

M
mates, 22

P
paws, 19
prey, 9, 16, 20

S
seals, 4, 6–7, 9, 16, 20
swimming, 18–19

T
teeth, 9

ANSWER KEY:
1. Answers will vary; 2. Answers will vary; 3. A; 4. B; 5. A; 6. C